The Details of the Rocket System

WILLIAM CONGREVE

The Details of the Rocket System

Employed by the British Army During the Napoleonic Wars

ILLUSTRATED

William Congreve

LEONAUR

The Details of the Rocket System
Employed by the British Army During the Napoleonic Wars
by William Congreve

ILLUSTRATED

First published under the title
The Details of the Rocket System

Leonaur is an imprint of Oakpast Ltd
Copyright in this form © 2021 Oakpast Ltd

ISBN: 978-1-78282-920-1 (hardcover)
ISBN: 978-1-78282-921-8 (softcover)

http://www.leonaur.com

Publisher's Notes

Contents

Introduction

His Royal Highness the Prince Regent, to whose gracious patronage the Rocket System owes its existence, having been pleased to command the formation of a Rocket Corps, on the 1st of January, 1814, by augmentation to the Regiment of Artillery, as proposed by his Lordship, the Earl of Mulgrave, Master General of the Ordnance; I have thought it my duty to draw up the following details of the System, for the Instruction of the Officers of the Corps, for the information of the General Officers of the British Army, and that of such departments as it is important for the good of the service, to make acquainted with the principles of this new branch of our naval and military means of offence and defence.

I have, indeed, conceived it the more incumbent upon me to prepare such a document for the use of the Rocket Corps, with as much expedition as possible, that nothing might be wanting on my part towards its completion, having been induced to decline the offer graciously made me of commanding it, with rank in the regiment of artillery; a decision, in which I trust I have sufficiently proved myself to have been actuated by the most sincere desire of manifesting my attachment to that regiment; as, however flattering the offer, it was sufficient gratification to me to have brought my labours to a consummation, which enabled me to leave the undivided benefit of this new corps in their possession: and to have succeeded in putting into their hands a weapon, which it is my greatest pride to have already seen adding to their laurels, in the plains of Leipsic, and on the banks of the Adour; a weapon, which has so early given them pledges of future and greater successes, and which I hope the following pages will evince to have already been brought to a state of organisation and perfection, at least commensurate with its age.

I will hope, also, that the further progress and extension of the powers of the Rocket System will be such as not to discredit the discernment of the enlightened prince, who first patronised it, or that of his lordship, the Master General, by whose protection it is now placed on a permanent establishment.

William Congreve

ROYAL ARTILLERY
MOUNTED ROCKETT CORPS.

General Instructions for the Use of Rockets

Both in the Field and in Bombardment, showing the Spirit of the System, and its comparative Powers and Facilities

It must be laid down as a maxim, that "the very essence and spirit of the Rocket System is the facility of firing a great number of rounds in a short time, or even instantaneously, with small means," arising from this circumstance, that the rocket is a species of fixed ammunition which does not require ordnance to project it; and which, where apparatus is required, admits of that apparatus being of the most simple and portable kind.

An officer, therefore, having the use of this weapon under his direction, must ever bear this maxim in mind—and his first consideration must be—to make his discharges against the enemy in as powerful volleys as he possibly can.

Thus—if the defence of a post be entrusted to him, and the ground be at all favourable, he will, independent of the regular apparatus he may have at his disposal, prepare what may be called rocket batteries, consisting of as many embrasures as his ground will admit; these embrasures being formed by turning up the sod, so as to give channels of direction four or five feet long, and three feet apart: by which a great number of rockets in a volley may evidently be arranged to defend any assailable point. In these embrasures, if liable to surprise, the rockets may be placed in readiness the vents not uncovered; though generally speaking, this is not necessary, as so short a time is required to place them—here and there one, only being in its embrasure.

In battle also, where there is not, of course, time to prepare the ground as above stated, but where it is tolerably level, he may, in addition to the apparatus he possesses, add to his fire by discharging, from the intervals of his frames or cars, rockets merely laid on the ground in the direction required: and, if an enemy be advancing upon him, there is, in fact, no limit to the volley he may be prepared thus to give, when at a proper distance, but the quantity of ammunition he possesses, the extension of his own ground, and the importance of the object to be fired at.

Under these limits, he may choose his volley from 50 to 500—a fire which, if judiciously laid in, must nearly annihilate his enemy: for this purpose, trains are provided. This practice also requires the exposure of only one or two men, who are to fire the volley, as the remainder, with the ammunition, may be under cover. And here it should be remarked, that the length of ranges, and the height of the curve of the *recochét*, in this mode of firing, depend on the length of the stick—the stick of the full length giving the longest range, but rising the highest from the ground; the reduced stick giving a shorter range, but keeping closer to the ground.

From this application, therefore, where practicable, by carrying a certain, number of the 12-pounder pouches in the ammunition waggon, an officer, even with a dismounted brigade, may always manoeuvre and detach parties to get upon the flanks of any approaching or fixed column, square, or battalion, while he himself remains with the heavier ammunition and cars in front.

This mode of firing from the ground of course applies only for moderate distances; the limits of which, with the smaller natures of rockets, may be considered from 800 to 1,000 yards, and for the larger from 1,000 to 1,200; where therefore greater ranges are required, the apparatus must be resorted to. And here it is proper to remark that in the use of the rocket, at least in the present state of the system, no certain increase of range can be depended upon by increasing the elevations from the ground-ranges up to 15°, for the smaller rockets; and 20° to 25° for the larger; for in the intermediate angles, the rocket is apt to drop in going off, and graze near the frame; but at the above angles it will always proceed in a single curve to very greatly increased ranges from 1,500 to 2,000 yards.

In bombardment, as well as in the field, the quantity of instantaneous fire is equally important, and the greater number of rockets that can be thrown, not only increase the number of fires, but by distracting the enemy's attention, prevent their extinction. To this end, therefore, an officer should always employ as many bombarding frames as possible; and here again he will find, that in bombardment, as well as in the field, the weapon affords him the means of extending his fire beyond the compass of his apparatus.

Thus, he may form a rocket battery of any common epaulement, parallel to the face of the town to be bombarded, by digging a trench in the rear of it to admit the stick, so as to lay the rocket and stick against the slope of the epaulement, that slope being brought to the desired elevation for projecting the rocket, or by boring holes to receive the stick; or he may construct a slope expressly as a rocket battery; and as, in firing these volleys, his rockets need not be more than three feet apart, it follows, that from an epaulement or battery of this description, fifty yards in length, he may keep up this bombardment by a discharge of fifty rockets in a volley, and repeat these volleys every five minutes if desirable; a rate of firing which must inevitably baffle all attempts of the most active and numerous enemy to prevent its effect.

It is obvious, therefore, that in any comparison made of the powers of the rocket with those of common artillery, whether an officer be called on merely to demonstrate its powers, or to carry it actually against an enemy, the foregoing maxim must be his rule; in fact, everything should be demonstrated according to the spirit of its use; a single rocket is not to be compared with a single gunshot, by firing it at a target. But the consideration is, whether for general service, the power of quantity in the fire of rockets does not *at least* counterbalance the greater accuracy of the gun? and for this purpose the spirit of the demonstration of the rocket system is to shew how few men are required to produce the most powerful volleys with this arm.

No demonstration should be made with less than twenty rounds in a volley; to maintain which, in any fixed position, at the rate of two or even three volleys a minute, twenty men may be said to be sufficient, and this with rockets projecting cohorn, or 5½-inch howitzer shells, or even 18- and 24-pounder solid shot. The first point of comparison therefore, is—How many rounds of such ammunition in the minute could twenty men project by the ordinary means of artillery?—or how many in a volley, even if they had all the means at hand?—And the next point is—what are the comparative facilities in bringing these different means into action, where the one system requires only the transport of the ammunition—the other, not only that of the ammunition, but of the most massive ordnance, without which it is entirely useless?

But independent of this comparison as to quantity, there are others in which the rocket has advantages exclusively its own: there are situations where artillery cannot by any means be brought into action, while there is no situation, no nature of ground, which is passable to an infantry soldier with his musket in his hand, that is not equally to be passed by the rocketteer with *his* arm and ammunition.

For the accomplishment of any particular service, he may dispense entirely with wheel carriages or even horses; there is nothing which the men themselves cannot transport and bring into action; and if any bombardment were required by a *coup de main*, 1,000 men would not only convey 1,000 rounds of the heaviest Carcass Rockets, a number sufficient to destroy any place within the compass of their range, but would perform that service in a few hours, having neither batteries or platforms to erect, nor mortars to convey.

Such are the true principles of this new system of artillery, for (projecting the same ammunition) so it may be called, and the greater the scale of equipment, the greater in proportion will its powers appear; thus, if an establishment were formed on the strength of a cavalry regiment, if 600 mounted men were equipped on the principles of the present detachment, they would take into action, without ammunition horses or wheel carriages, 2,400 rounds of ammunition, and 200 *abouches a feù*; and if 100 ammunition horses were attached to this corps, it would further possess a reserve of nearly 2,000 rounds more; the whole capable of every movement and service practicable by any other regiment of heavy cavalry; and the same proportionate power would be found to attach to every other mode of equipment.

In addition to this view of the powers of the weapon, it is important to state, that the detail of the service is most extraordinarily simple; that there are but a few points to be attended to in its application; and those such as may be most easily acquired; the principal ones are, that care must be taken to fix the sticks very firmly to the rocket, and in the true direction of the axis of the rocket, to prevent aberration of flight.

That, at high angles, the frame must always be elevated for the large rockets from 5° to 10° more than the elevation at which the rocket is intended to be projected, and in the small rockets from 2½° to 5°; for, as the rocket leaves the frame before it has obtained its full force, it drops a certain number of degrees in proportion to its weight at going off. Thus, the longest ranges of the 32-poundcr Carcass Rockets are obtained at about 55°, or rather more, if the rockets have been long made. An officer, however, being prepared for this circumstance, will soon discover the maximum range of the rockets he may have to discharge.

Some allowance in elevation also must be made for the direction of the wind; if it is powerful, and blows in a contrary direction to that in which the rocket is projected, the frame requires more elevation; for the wind acting more on the stick than the body of the rocket, depresses the elevation in its rising. If on the contrary, it blows in the direction of the rocket's flight, *less* elevation is required; for, in this case, the rocket mounts by the wind's action on the stick.

So, from the same cause, if the wind be strong, and across the range, though no difference of elevation is necessary, still an allowance must be made to leeward; for the rocket, contrary to the course of ordinary projectiles, has a tendency to draw to windward: a few rounds however, in all these cases, will immediately point out to the observant officer what is the required allowance.

These remarks refer only to high angles; for no effect whatever is produced by the wind in the ground-ranges: in these the only caution necessary to be attended to is, to choose the most smooth and level spot for the first 100 yards in front of the point from which it is intended to discharge these rockets, as they generally travel in contact with the surface for this distance, not having acquired their full force, and are therefore more liable to deflection; but having at this point acquired a velocity not much less than the mean velocity of a cannon ball, they are not to be more easily deflected.

At this distance also they rise a few feet from the ground, so as to clear any ordinary obstacles that may occur; insomuch that, if it were desired to fire rockets at low angles into a besieged town, from the third parallel, these rockets, having a clear space to acquire their velocity, in front of the parallel, would run up the glacis, clear the ditch, and skim over the parapet into the town; and would no doubt be of great use in a variety of cases, particularly in discomfiting and rendering the enemy unsteady, by pouring in volleys of some hundreds or even thousands on this principle, previous to an assault or escalade: indeed, knowing the effect, I do not hesitate to affirm that this manoeuvre, practised on *the great scale*, would infallibly dislodge any enemy posted for the protection of a breach.

Sufficient has, I conceive, now been stated, to give the officer such a general view of the power and spirit of the weapon, as may enable him to apply it in all possible cases to the best advantage; and if he will but constantly bear in view that maxim which I have laid down as the fundamental principle of this system, I will confidently pledge myself that it will never disappoint him, either as to the physical or *moral* effect which he may calculate on producing upon his enemy; since, he must recollect, that for this latter effect, it adds all the terrors of *visibility* to every species of that destructive ammunition introduced by the use of gun-powder, but by everyone admitted hitherto to have been qualified, as to moral effect, by its *invisibility*.

W. Congreve.

25th October, 1813.

Note.—All the cases of service referred to in the above instructions, will be found particularly detailed in the following plates.

Constitution and Strength of a Troop of Rocket Horse Artillery

A troop is proposed to consist of three divisions.

Each division to be divided into two sub-divisions.

Each sub-division to consist of five sections of three men each, and two drivers leading four ammunition horses, each mounted man carrying into action four rounds of 12-pounder rocket ammunition, and each ammunition horse eighteen rounds; thus:

Each section carries 12 rounds of ammunition into action, and one *bouche a feù*, and, consequently, each sub-division will have five *bouches a feù*, and 140 rounds of ammunition: so that the whole troop, consisting of six of those sub-divisions, will amount to 102 mounted men, and 24 ammunition horses, and will take into action, without any wheel carriage, 30 *bouches a feù*, and 840 rounds of ammunition.

It is, however, further proposed to attach to each division two rocket cars, one heavy and one light, the first carrying four men with 40 rounds of 24-pounder rockets, armed with cohorn shells, the latter carrying two men, and 60 rounds of 12-pounder ammunition. Each of these cars is capable of discharging two rockets in a volley.

It is proposed, also, to attach to each sub-division a curricle ammunition cart, or tumbril, for two horses, to carry, in line of march, three rounds out of four of each mounted man's rockets, to ease the horse: and, in action, when every man carries his full complement of ammunition on horseback, these cars may contain a reserve of 60 rounds more for each sub-division, making

An OFFICER, PRIVATE & DRIVER of the
ROYAL WAGGON TRAIN.

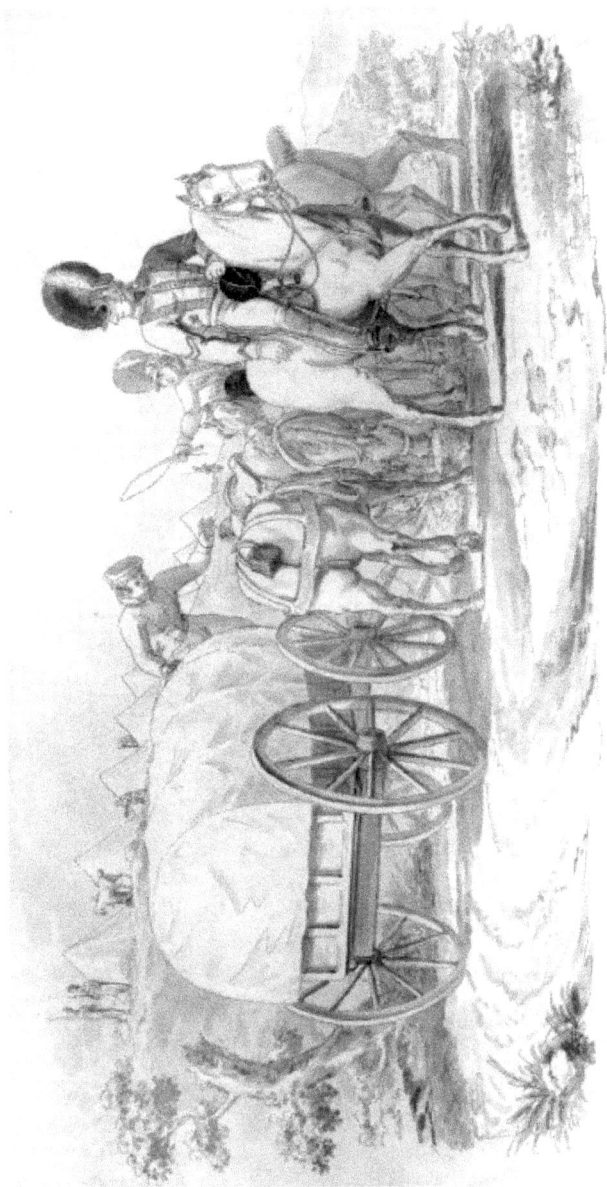

Royal Artillery Drivers

the whole amount of ammunition, for each sub-division, 200 rounds. With this addition, therefore, the whole strength of the rocket troop will stand thus:

Officers	5
Non-commissioned Officers	15
Troopers	90
Drivers	60
Artificers	8
Cars, heavy	3
Cars, light	3
Curricle ammunition carts, or tumbrils	6
Bouches a feù	42
Ammunition, heavy shell	260
Ditto light shell, or case shot	1200

Making a total of:—

Ammunition of all sorts	1460 rounds
Battery of	42 *bouches a feù*
Cars, tumbrils, and forge cart	13
Officers, staff artificers, troopers, and drivers	172
Troop, ammunition, and draft horses	164

The number of sections in a sub-division may vary according to the actual effective strength of the troop at any time; so that the distribution may be accommodated to the numbers, without departing from this principle of constitution. The number of men and horses above stated is precisely the same as that of a troop of horse artillery.

The reserve of ammunition is supposed to proceed with the park.

The Equipment of Rocket Cavalry

Plate 1 represents the mode of equipment for carrying rockets on horseback, as it was arranged during the course of experiments, which were carried on, under my direction, at Bagshot, in 1811; as it was subsequently carried into actual service, under Captain Bogle, with the Allied armies in Germany, in the ever memorable campaign of 1813; and as it is at present proposed to equip the new corps of Rocket Horse Artillery, established on the 1st of January, 1814, by Earl Mulgrave, Master General of the Ordnance, and composed of two troops, under the command of Lieutenant Colonel Fisher, of the Royal Artillery.

The right hand figure represents a trooper completely armed and equipped, in review order. The left hand figure is a delineation of the same, with the *shabracque* removed, to shew the holsters in which the rockets are conveyed. These holsters each contain two 12-pounder rockets, each rocket armed with a 6-pounder shell, or case shot; they are connected together at top, and are supported by the pummel of the saddle, which is made in the hussar fashion, though the saddle itself is, in fact, formed and stuffed the same as a common English saddle.

This projection in front keeps the holsters clear of the horse's withers and shoulders, which, from their size, it might otherwise be difficult to do; for the latter of these purposes, also, the flap of the saddle comes further forward than usual. The holsters, thus connected, slip on and off from the pummel with great facility, which is an object of importance, as a part of the service of the rocket trooper is, when from some impassable obstacle, he can

Plate 1

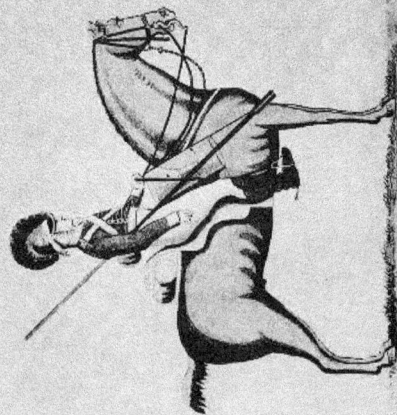

ROYAL HORSE ARTILLERY OFFICER, 1820

no longer advance on horseback, to dismount and pass over such obstacle, with his ammunition holsters and chamber, on foot. The sticks, which are seven feet in length, and four in number, answering to the number of rockets, are collected in a bundle by means of a strap with four loops, contrived on purpose, and are carried on the off-side, the thicker ends being supported in a bucket, suspended from the flap of the saddle.

The strap above mentioned, as confining them together in the middle, leading across the man's thigh to the peak of the saddle; by this means they fall naturally under his right arm, without at all incommoding him, either in mounting or dis-mounting, or even in going through the sword exercise. By this arrangement also, they are easily drawn from the bundle down-wards, for fixing to the rocket, leaving any number that may remain as securely fixed as when the whole are in the quiver.

It has already been stated, that the men are told off in sec-tions of threes. They are accordingly numbered 1, 2, and 3. Now numbers 1 and 3 have nothing to carry but their proportion of the ammunition, *viz.* four rockets and four sticks each, while No. 2 has in addition to carry the chamber from which the rockets of his section are discharged. This chamber is a small iron plate trough, about one foot six inches in length, capable of being fixed steadily in the ground by four iron points at the bottom of it, so that the rockets may be discharged parallel to the surface and close to it. The weight of this chamber, or *bouche a feù*, is about six lbs. and it is carried in a small leather case, shewn in both these figures, just at the back of the valise.

The men are armed with a sabre, which is in action suspend-ed to the saddle, that they may not be incumbered in mounting and dismounting. Each man has besides a pistol in his cross belt, and a spear head in his holster, which may be occasionally fixed at the end of one of the rocket sticks, so as to give the further aid of a very formidable lance.

Instead of carrying slow match, which would be dangerous as well as inconvenient, the portfire is lighted in action by a flash of powder obtained from a pistol lock and pan, mounted on a small stock; and a light portfire stick for discharging the rocket, about three feet in length, is constructed of a thin iron tube, which shuts up, and is carried in the holster. The sticks are fastened in the loops on the rocket case, either by the gripe of a pair of pincers with points in them, or by the stroke of a small hammer with a point in the head, or by some equally simple tool. Every part of this equipment, except the sticks, is so completely concealed by the *shabracque*, that the rocket trooper has the appearance merely of a lancer.

The weight of ammunition carried by the troop horse, with the full complement going into action, is three stone six lbs.; to which the horse is fully equal for any ordinary operation. But in long marches, it would be not only useless but improvident to burthen him to this extent; small tumbrils, therefore, are provided to convey three rounds of each man's rockets, he still carrying one round on the near side, and the four sticks on the off side to balance, which leaves the horse, in travelling, only one stone four lbs. weight of ammunition to carry; a burthen of two stone less on line of march, than that of the heavy dragoon's or artillery man's horse; allowing for the difference of the weight of the men requisite for the respective services.

The rocket trooper has no heavy weights to lift—no guns to spunge, or to limber up and unlimber. He is required merely to be light and active for mounting and dismounting, and for moving nimbly on foot with a single rocket, when in action: so that, whereas an artillery man cannot average less than 13 stone, the rocket trooper need not exceed 10 stone, a difference amounting within a few pounds to the whole weight of ammunition carried by the men, even in action. It is needless to add that this difference in the men must also give great facility in recruiting for a rocket corps.

Plate 2 represents the mode of equipping the Ammunition Horses.

The left hand figure shews that the whole of the ammunition, &c. may be completely covered and protected from the weather by a painted canvass; and the other has this cover off, to shew the particular distribution of the load, which consists of eighteen rockets and rocket sticks, and a proportion of small

Plate 2

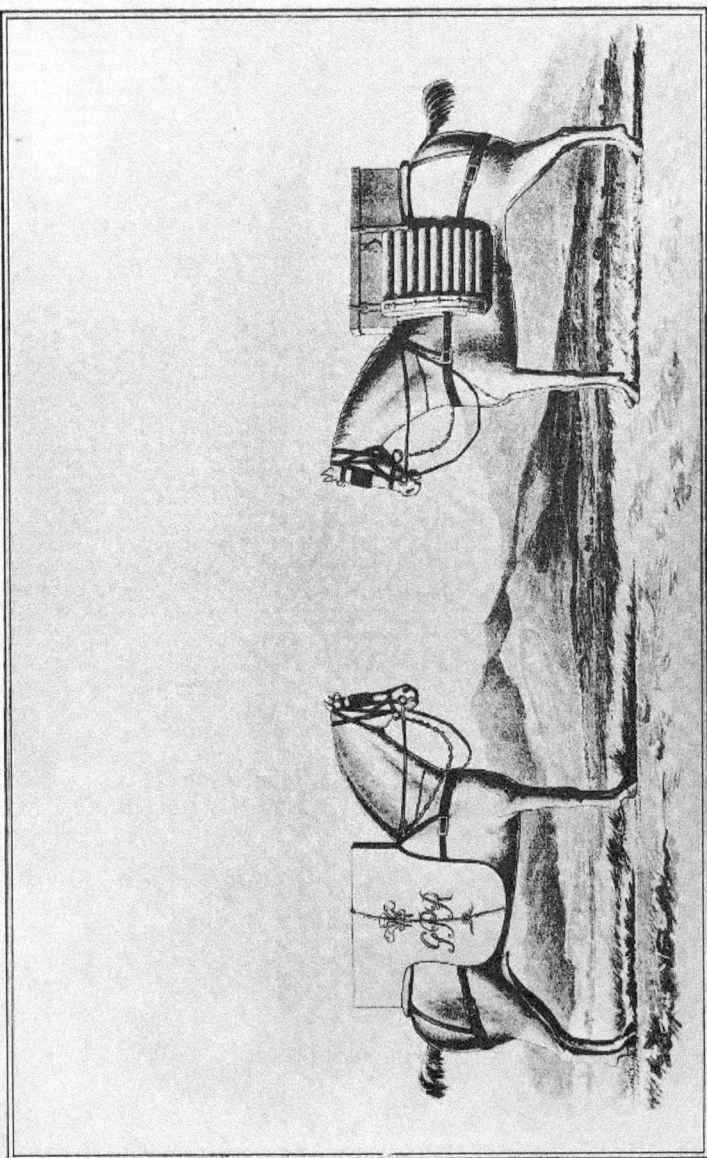

stores, such as portfires, slow match, &c.

This load is carried on a bat saddle, made as small and as light as possible, with a pad at the back part of it, extending towards the crupper. The saddle is furnished on the top with two iron forks to receive a leather case, in which the sticks are carried in half lengths, of three feet six inches each, a length from which no inconvenience arises; being contrived so that the two parts may be united, to form the stick complete in a moment, by means of a ferule fixed to one end and receiving the other; in which situation they are firmly fixed and connected, either by a pair of pointed pincers, by a hammer with a point in the head, or by a wrench. When these sticks are taken from the ammunition horse, to replenish the stock of the mounted men, they are to be joined at that, time by the simple, secure, and momentary operation just mentioned.

The rockets are carried in a sort of saddle bags, as they may be termed, stitched into separate compartments for each rocket, covered by a flap at one end, and secured by a chain, staples, and padlocks, the rocket lying horizontally. By this arrangement the load lies in the most compact form possible, and close to the horse's side, while the rockets, being thus separated, cannot be injured by carriage.

The load is divided into three parts, the case or bundle of eighteen sticks, and a separate saddle bag on each side, contrived to hook on to the saddle, carrying nine rockets in each bag. By this means there is no difficulty in loading and unloading the horse.

The whole weight thus carried by an Ammunition Horse is about 19 stone, consisting of about 6½ stone for the saddle, sticks, &c. and about six stone in each of the saddlebags. From which it is evident, that there is no fear of the load swagging the horse in travelling, because the centre of gravity is very considerably below his back bone. It is evident also, that as the weight of the rockets diminishes by supplying the mounted men, the weight of the sticks also is diminished, and the centre of gravity may, if desired, be brought lower and lower, as the load diminishes, by taking the ammunition from the upper tiers gradually and equally on each side downwards. It is further evident, that although spaces are provided for nine rockets in each bag, that number may be diminished, should the difficulty of the country, or the length of the march, or other circumstances, render it advisable to carry a less load.

The mode of leading these horses will be explained in the next plate.

ROCKET TROOPER

Reitendes Raketeur-Corps
(Royal Artillery. Mounted Rockett Corps.)

Reitende Artillerie
(Royal Horse Artillery.)

1813.

Rocket Cavalry in Line of March, and in Action

Plate 3, Fig. 1, represents a sub-division of Rocket Cavalry, or Rocket Horse Artillery, marching in column of threes. It consists of six sections, of three men in each, or a less number of sections, according to the whole strength of the troop, followed by four ammunition horses, each pair led by a driver riding between them; on the full scale, therefore, a sub-division will consist of 24 horses and 20 men, and will carry into action 152 rounds of 12-pounder Shell or Case Shot Rockets, and six *bouches a feù* or chambers, carried by the centre men of each section.

Fig. 2 represents this division in action, where the division may be supposed to have been halted in line, on the words—*"Prepare for action it? front—dismount"*—Nos. 1 and 3 having dismounted, and given their leading reins to No. 2, who remains mounted, No. 1 runs forward about 15 or 20 paces with the chamber, which he draws from the leather case at the back of No. 2's valise; and while Nos. 2 and 3 are preparing a rocket, drawn from any one of the holsters most convenient, No. 1 fixes the chamber into the ground, pointing it to the desired object, and lights his portfire ready for the first round, which No. 3 by this time will have brought to him, and laid into the chamber.

There remains, then, only for No. 1 to touch the vent of the rocket with his portfire, No. 3 having run back for another round, which No. 2 will have been able to prepare in the mean-time. In this way the sub-division will, without hurry, come into action with six *bouches a feù* , in one minute's time, and may continue their fire, without any extraordinary exertion, at the rate of from two to three rounds from each chamber in a minute, or even four with good exertion; so that the six *bouches a feù* would discharge 80 rounds of 6-pounder ammunition in three minutes. Twelve light frames for firing the 12-pounder rockets at high angles are further provided in addition to the ground chambers, and each of the drivers of the ammunition horses has one in his charge, in case of distant action.

The preparation of the rocket for firing is merely the fixing the stick to it, either by the pincers, pointed hammer, or wrench, provided for joining the parts of the stick also. These modes I have lately devised, as being more simple and economical than the screw formerly used; but cannot at present pronounce which is the best; great care, however, must be taken to fix the stick securely, as everything depends on it; the vent also must be very carefully uncovered, as, if not perfectly so, the rocket is liable to burst; and in firing the portfire must not be thrust too far into the rocket, for the same reason.

On the words "*Cease firing,*" No. 1 cuts his portfire, takes up his chamber, runs back to his section, and replaces the chamber immediately. No. 3 also immediately runs back; and having no other operation to perform, replaces the leading reins, and the whole are ready to mount again, for the performance of any further manoeuvre that may be ordered, in less than a minute from the word "*Cease firing*" having been given.

It is obvious that the combined celerity and quantity of the discharge of ammunition of this description of artillery cannot be equalled or even approached, taking in view the means and nature of ammunition employed, by any other known system; the universality also of the operation, not being incumbered with wheel carriages, must be duly appreciated, as, in fact, it can proceed not only wherever cavalry can act, but even wherever infantry can get into action; it having been already mentioned that part of the exercise of these troops, supposing them to be stopped by walls, or ditches and morasses, impassable to horses, is to take the holsters and sticks from the horses, and advance on foot.

Plate 3

Fig. 1

Fig. 2

Another vast advantage is the few men required to make a complete section, as by this means the number of points of fire is so greatly multiplied, compared to any other system of artillery. Thus it may be stated that the number of *bouches a feù*, which may comparatively be brought into action, by equal means, on the scale of a troop of horse artillery, would be at least six to one; and that they may either be spread over a great extent of line, or concentrated into a very small focus, according to the necessity of the service; indeed the skirmishing exercise of the Rocket Cavalry, divided and spread into separate sections, and returning by sound of bugle, forms a very interesting part of the system, and can be well imagined from the foregoing description and the plate.

Rocket Cars

Plate 4, Fig. 1, represents a Rocket Car in line of march. There are two descriptions of these cars, of similar construction—one for 32 or 24-pounder ammunition, the other for 18 or 12-pounder; and which are, therefore, called heavy or light cars: the heavy car will carry 40 rounds of 24-pounder rockets, armed with cohorn shells, and the light one will convey 60 rounds of 12-pounder, or 50 of 18-pounder ammunition, which is packed in boxes on the limber, the sticks being carried in half lengths in the boxes on the after part of the carriage, where the men also ride on seats fixed for the purpose, and answering also for small store boxes; they are each supposed to be drawn by four horses.

These cars not only convey the ammunition, but are contrived also to discharge each two rockets in a volley from a double iron plate trough, which is of the same length as the boxes for the sticks, and travels between them; but which, being moveable, may, when the car is unlimbered, be shifted into its fighting position at any angle from the ground ranges, or point blank up to 45°, without being detached from the carnage.

Fig. 2 represents these rocket cars in action: the one on the left hand has its trough in the position for ground firing, the trough being merely lifted off the bed of the axle tree on which it travels, and laid on the ground, turning by two iron stays on a centre in the axle tree; the right hand car is elevated to a high angle, the trough being raised and supported by the iron stays behind, and in front by the perch of the carriage, connected to

Plate 4

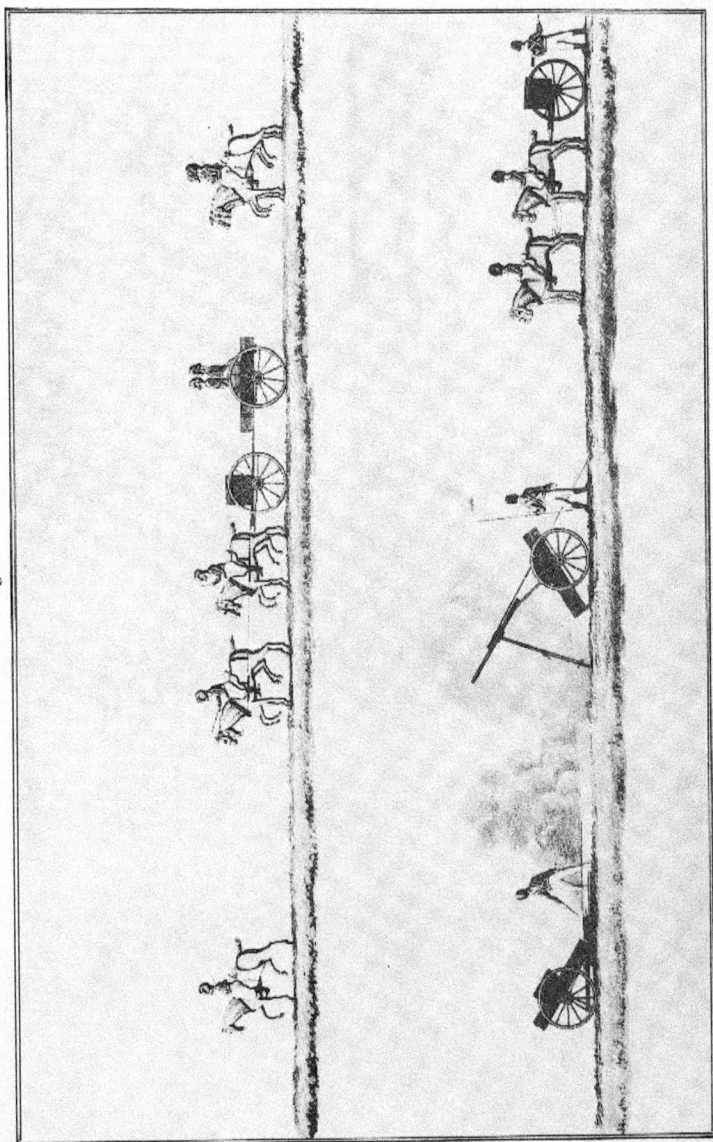

Fig. 1

Fig. 2

it by a joint, the whole kept steady by bolting the stays, and by tightening a chain from the perch to the axle tree. The limbers are always supposed to be in the rear. The rockets are fired with a portfire and long stick; and two men will fight the light car, four men the heavy one.

The exercise is very simple; the men being told off, Nos. 1, 2, 3, and 4, to the heavy carriage. On the words, "*Prepare for action, and unlimber*" the same process takes place as in the 6-pounder exercise. On the words, "*Prepare for ground firing*" Nos. 2 and 3 take hold of the hand irons, provided on purpose, and, with the aid of No. 4, raise the trough from its travelling position, and lower it down to the ground under the carriage; or on the words "*Prepare to elevate*" raise it to the higher angles, No. 4 bolting the stays, and fixing the chain. No. 1 having in the meantime prepared and lighted his portfire, and given the direction of firing to the trough, Nos. 2, 3, and 4, then run to the limber to fix the ammunition, which No. 2 brings up, two rounds at a time, or one, as ordered, and helping No. 1 to place them in the trough as far back as the stick will admit.

This operation is facilitated by No. 1 stepping upon the lower end of either of the stick boxes, on which a cleat is fastened for this purpose; No. 1 then discharges the two rockets separately, firing that to leeward first, while No. 2 returns for more ammunition: this being the hardest duty, the men will, of course, relieve No. 2 in their turns. In fighting the light frame, two men are sufficient to elevate or depress it, but they will want aid to fix and bring up the ammunition for quick firing.

Rocket Infantry in Line of March, and in Action

Plate 5, Fig. 1, represents a sub-division of rocket infantry in line of march—Fig. 2, the same, in action. The system here shewn is the use of the rockets by infantry—one man in ten, or any greater proportion, carrying a frame, of very simple construction, from which the rockets may be discharged either for ground ranges, or at high angles, and the rest carrying each three rounds of ammunition, which, for this service, is proposed to be either the 12-pounder shell rockets, or the 12-pounder rocket case shot, each round equal to the 6-pounder case, and ranging 2,500 yards. So that 100 men will bring into action, in any situation where musketry can be used, nearly 300 rounds of this description of artillery, with ranges at 45°, double those of light held ordnance.

The exercise and words of command are as follow:

No. 1 carries the frame, which is of very simple construction, standing on legs like a theodolite, when spread, and which closes similarly for carrying. This frame requires no spunging, the rocket being fired merely from an open cradle, from which it may be either discharged by a lock or by a portfire, in which case. No. 1 also carries the pistol, portfire-lighter, and tube box. No. 2 carries a small pouch, with the requisite small stores, such as spare tubes, portfires, &c.; and a long portfire stick.

Nos. 3, 4, and 5, &c. to 10, carry each, conveniently, on his back, a pouch, containing three rockets; and three sticks, secured together by straps and buckles.

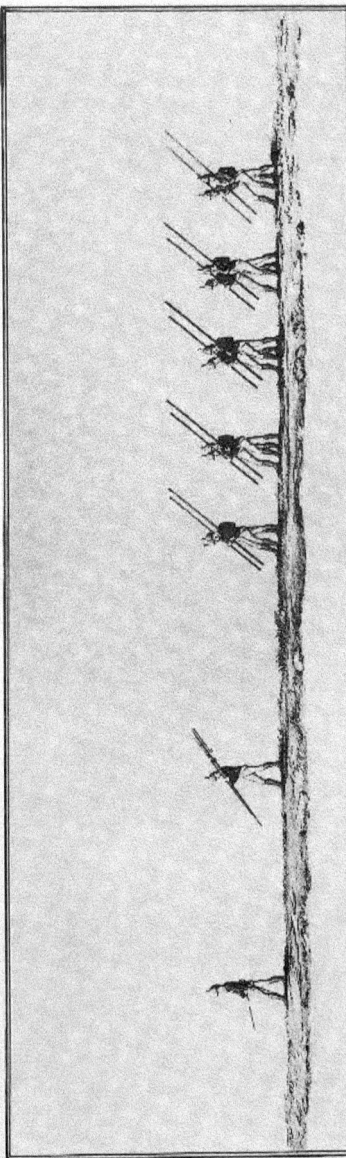

Plate 5

Fig. 1

Fig. 2

With this distribution, they advance in double files. On the word "*Halt*," "*Prepare for action*" being given, No. 1 spreads his frame, and with the assistance of No. 2, fixes it firmly into the ground, preparing it at the desired elevation. No. 2 then hands the portfire stick to No. 1, who prepares and lights it, while No. 2 steps back to receive the rocket; which has been prepared by Nos. 3, 4, &c. who have fallen back about fifteen paces, on the word being given to "*Prepare for action*." These men can always supply the ammunition quicker than it can be fired, and one or other must therefore advance towards the frame to meet No. 2 with the round prepared.

No. 2 having thus received the rocket, places it on the cradle, at the same instant that No. 1 puts a tube into the vent. No. 2 then joints the frame, which has an universal traverse after the legs are fixed; he then gives the word "*Ready*" "*Fire*," to No. 1, who takes up his portfire and discharges the rocket. No. 1 now sticks his portfire stick into the ground, and prepares another tube; while No. 2, as before, puts the rocket into the frame, points, and gives the word "*Ready*," "*Fire*." again.

By this process, from three to four rockets a minute may, without difficulty, be fired from one frame, until the words "*Cease firing*," "*Prepare to advance*." or "*retreat*," are given; when the frame is in a moment taken front the ground, and the whole party may either retire or advance immediately in press time, if required.

To insure which, and at the same time to prevent any injury to the ammunition, Nos. 3, 4, &.c. must not be allowed to take off their pouches, as they will be able to assist one another in preparing the ammunition, by only laying down their sticks; in taking up which again no time is lost. If the frame is fired with a lock, the same process is used, except that No. 1 primes and cocks, and No. 2 fires on receiving the word from No. I.

For ground firing, the upper part of this frame, consisting of the chamber and elevating stem, takes off from the legs, and the bottom of the stem being pointed like a picquet post, forms a very firm *bouche a feù* when stuck into the ground; the chamber at point blank being at a very good height for this practice, and capable of traversing in any direction. The exercise, in this case, is, of course, in other respects similar to that at high angles.

The Mode of Using Rockets in Bombardment

Plate 6, Fig. 1, represents the mode of carrying the bombard-ing frame and ammunition by men. The apparatus required is merely a light ladder, 12 feet in length, having two iron cham-bers, which are fixed on in preparing for action at the upper end of the ladder; from which chambers the rockets are discharged, by means of a musket lock; the ladder being reared to any eleva-tion, by two legs or pry-poles, as in Fig. 2.

Everything required for this service may be carried by men; or a Flanders-pattern ammunition waggon, with four horses, will convey 60 rounds of 32-pounder carcasses, in ten boxes, eight of the boxes lying cross-ways on the floor of the waggon, and two lengthways, at top. On these the frame, complete for firing two rockets at a flight, with spunges, &c. is laid; and the sticks on each side, to complete the stowage of all that is nec-essary, the whole being covered by the tilt. Four men only are required to be attached to each waggon, who are numbered 1, 2, 3, & 4.

The frame and ammunition having been brought into the battery, or to any other place, concealed either by trees or houses (for from the facility of taking new ground, batteries are not so indispensable as with mortars), the words "*Prepare for bombard-ment*" are given; on which the frame is prepared for rearing, Nos. 1 and 2 first fixing the chambers on the ladder; Nos. 3 and 4 at-taching the legs to the frame as it lies on the ground. The words "*Rear frame*" are then given; when all assist in raising it, and the proper elevation is given, according to the words "*Elevate to 35°*"

or "45°," or whatever angle the officer may judge necessary, according to the required range, by spreading or closing the legs of the frame, agreeable to the distances marked in degrees on a small measuring tape, which the non-commissioned officer carries, and which is called—the Elevating Line. The word "*Point*" is then given: which is done by means of a plumb-line, hanging down from the vertex of the triangle, and which at the same time shews whether the frame is upright or not.

Things being thus arranged, Nos. 1 and 2 place themselves at the foot of the ladder, and Nos. 3 and 4 return to fix the ammunition in the rear, in readiness for the word "*Load.*" When this is given, No. 3 brings a rocket to the foot of the ladder, having beforehand *carefully* taken off the circle that covered the vent, and handing it to No. 2, runs for another.

In the meantime, No. 1 has ascended the ladder to receive the first rocket from No. 2, and to place it in the chamber at the top of the ladder; by the time this is done, No. 2 is ready to give him another rocket, which in like manner he places in the other chamber: he then primes the locks with a tube and powder, and, cocking the two locks, after everything else is done, descends from the ladder, and, when down, gives the word "*Ready;*" on which, he and No. 2 each take one of the trigger lines, and retire ten or twelve paces obliquely, waiting for the word "*Fire*" from the officer or non-commissioned officer, on which they pull, either separately or together, as previously ordered.

On the rockets leaving the frame, No. 1 immediately runs up and spunges out the two chambers with a very wet spunge, having for this purpose a water bucket suspended at the top of the frame; which being done, he receives a rocket from No. 2, as before, No. 3 having, in the meantime, brought up a fresh supply; in doing which, however, he must never bring from the rear more than are wanted for each round. In this routine, any number of rounds is fired, until the words "*Cease firing*" are given; which, if followed by those, "*Prepare to retreat,*" Nos. 3 and 4 run forward to the ladder; and on the words "*Lower frame,*" they ease it down in the same order in which it was raised, take it to pieces, and may thus retire in less than five minutes: or if the object of ceas-

Plate 6

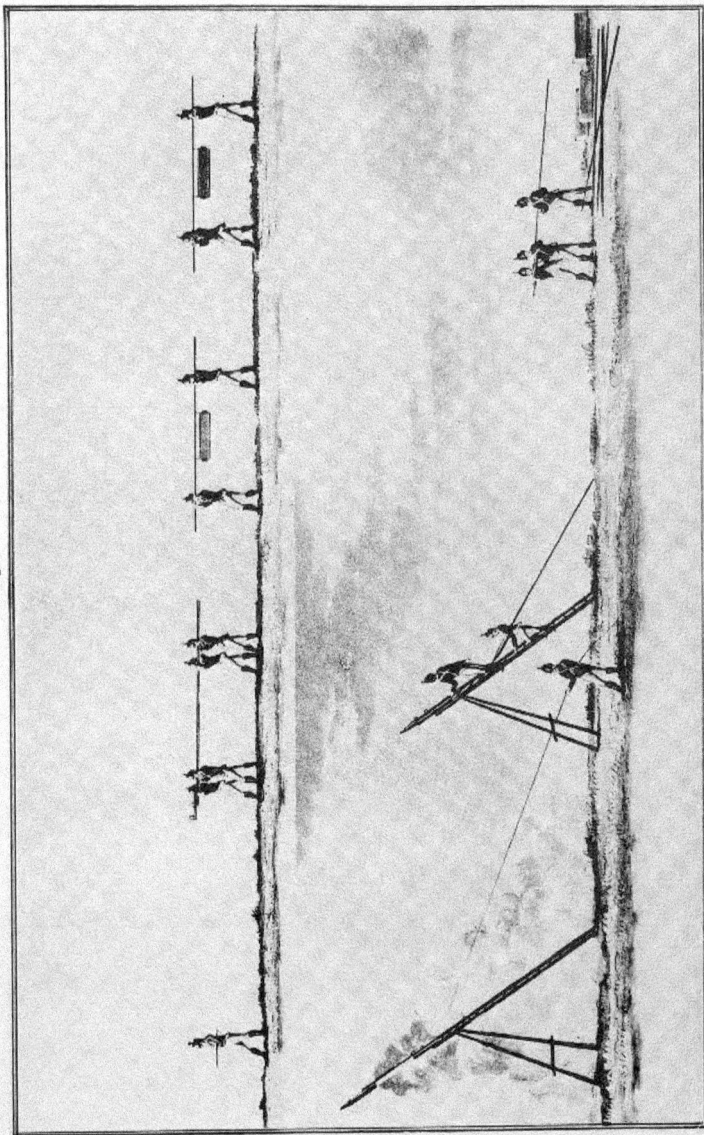

Fig. 1

Fig. 2

ing to fire is merely a change of position to no great distance, the four men may with ease carry the frame, without taking it to pieces, the waggon following them with the ammunition, or the ammunition being borne by men, as circumstances may render expedient.

The ammunition projected from this frame consists of 32-pounder rockets, armed with carcasses of the following sorts and ranges:—

1st.—*The small carcass*, containing 8 lbs. of carcass composition, being 3 lbs. more than the present 10-inch spherical carcass.—Range 3,000 yards.

2nd.—*The medium carcass*, containing 12 lbs. of carcass composition, being equal to the present 13-inch.—Range 2,500 yards.

3rd.—*The large carcass*, containing 18 lbs. of carcass composition, being 6 lbs. more than the present 13-inch spherical carcass.—Range 2,000 yards.

Or 32-pounder rockets, armed with bursting cones, made of stout iron, filled with powder, to be exploded by fuses, and to be used to produce the explosive effects of shells, where such effect is preferred to the conflagration of the carcass. These cones contain as follows:—

Small.—Five lbs. of powder, equal to the bursting powder of a 10-inch shell.—Range 3,000 yards.

Medium.—Eight lbs. of powder, equal to the bursting powder of a 13-inch shell.
Range 2,500 yards.

Large.—Twelve lbs. of powder.—Range 2,000 yards.

N.B. I have lately had a successful experiment, with bombarding rockets, six inches diameter, and weighing 148 lbs.— and doubt not of extending the bombarding powers of the system much further.

The Mode of Using Rockets in Bombardment, from Earth Works, without Apparatus

Plate 7, Fig. 1, is a perspective view of a battery, erected expressly for throwing rockets in bombardment, where the interior slope has the angle of projection required, and is equal to the length of the rocket and stick.

The great advantage of this system is, that, as it dispenses with apparatus: where there is time for forming a work of this sort, of considerable length, the quantity of fire, that may be thrown in a given time, is limited only by the length of the work: thus, as the rockets may be laid in embrasures cut in the bank, at every two feet, a battery of this description, 200 feet in length, will fire 100 rockets in a volley, and so on; or an incessant and heavy fire may, by such a battery, be kept up from one flank to the other, by replacing the rockets as fast as they are fired in succession.

The rule for forming this battery is as follows.

The length of the interior slope of this work is half formed by the excavation, and half by the earth thrown out; for the base therefore of the interior slope of the part to be. raised, at an angle of 55°, set off two thirds of the intended perpendicular height—cut down the slope to a perpendicular depth equal to the above mentioned height—then setting off, for the breadth of the interior excavation, one third more than the intended thickness of the work, carry down a regular ramp from the back part of this excavation

Plate 7

Fig. 1

Fig. 2

to the foot of the slope, and the excavation will supply the quantity of earth necessary to give the exterior face a slope of 45°.

Fig. 2 is a perspective view of a common epaulement converted into a rocket battery. In this case, as the epaulement is not of sufficient length to support the rocket and stick, holes must be bored in the ground, with a miner's borer, of a sufficient depth to receive the sticks, and at such distances, and such an angle, as it is intended to place the rockets for firing. The inside of the epaulement must be pared away to correspond with this angle, say 55°. The rockets are then to be laid in embrasures, formed in the bank, as in the last case. Where the ground is such as to admit of using the borer, this latter system, of course, is the easiest operation; and for such ground as would be likely to crumble into the holes, slight tubes are provided, about two feet long, to preserve the opening; in fact, these tubes will be found advantageous in all ground.

Fig. 2 also shews a powerful mode of defending a field work by means of rockets, in addition to the defences of the present system; merely by cutting embrasures in the glacis, for horizontal firing.

A Rocket Ambuscade

Plate 8, Fig. 1, represents one of the most important uses that can be made of rockets for field service; it is that of the Rocket Ambuscade for the defence of a pass, or for covering the retreat of an army, by placing any number, hundreds or thousands, of 32 or 24-pounder shell rockets, or of 32-pounder rockets, armed with 18-pounder shot, limited as to quantity only by the importance of the object, which is to be obtained; as by this means, the most extensive destruction, even amounting to annihilation, may be carried amongst the ranks of an advancing enemy, and that with the exposure of scarcely an individual.

The rockets are laid in rows or batteries of 100 or 500 in a row, according to the extent of ground to be protected. They are to be concealed either in high grass, or masked in any other convenient way; and the ambuscade may be formed of any required number of these batteries, one behind the other, each battery being prepared to be discharged in a volley, by leaders of quick match: so that one man is, in fact, alone sufficient to fire the whole in succession, beginning with that nearest to the enemy, as soon as he shall have perceived them near enough to warrant his firing.

Where the batteries are very extensive, each battery may be sub-divided into smaller parts, with separate trains to each, so that the whole, or any particular division of each battery, may be fired, according to the number and position of the enemy advancing. Trains, or leaders, are provided for this service, of a particular construction, being a sort of flannel *saucissons*, with two or three threads of slow match, which will strike laterally at

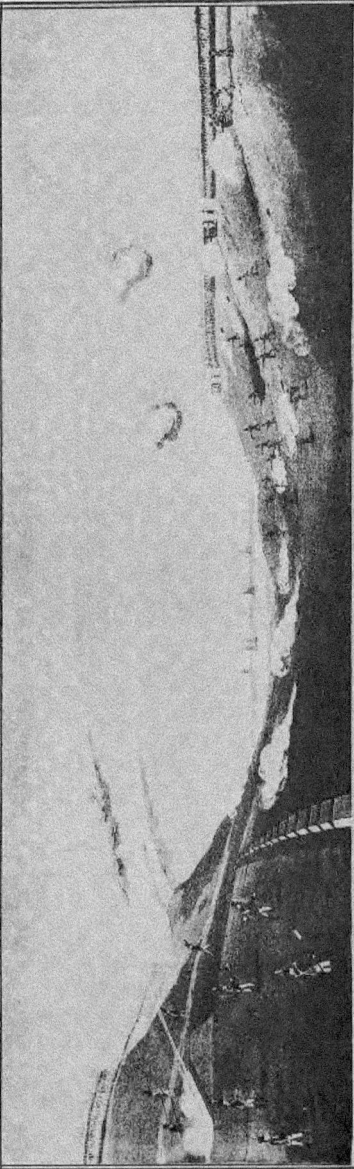

Plate 8

Fig. 1

Fig. 2

all points, and are therefore very easy of application; requiring only to be passed from rocket to rocket, crossing the vents, by which arrangement the fire running along, from vent to vent, is sure to strike every rocket in quick succession, without their disturbing each others' direction in going off, which they might otherwise do, being placed within 18 inches apart, if all were positively fired at the same instant.

Fig. 2 is a somewhat similar application, but not so much in the nature of an ambuscade as of an open defence. Here a very low work is thrown up, for the defence of a post, or of a chain of posts, consisting merely of as much earth and turf as is sufficient to form the sides of shallow embrasures for the large rockets, placed from two to three feet apart, or nearer; from which the rockets are supposed to be discharged independently, by a certain number of artillery-men, employed to keep up the fire, according to the necessity of the case.

It is evident, that by this mode, an incessant and tremendous fire may be maintained, which it would be next to impossible for an advancing enemy to pass through, not only from its quantity and the weight and destructive nature of the ammunition, but from the closeness of its lines and its contiguity to the ground; leaving, in fact, no space in front which must not be passed over and ploughed up after very few rounds.

As both these operations are supposed to be employed in defensive warfare, and therefore in fixed stations, there is no difficulty involved in the establishment of a sufficient depot of ammunition for carrying them on upon the most extensive scale; though it is obviously impossible to accomplish anything approaching this system of defence, by the ordinary means of artillery.

The Use of Rockets in the Attack and Defence of Fortified Places

Plate 9, Fig. 1, represents the advanced batteries and approaches in the attack of some fortress, where an imperfect breach being supposed to have been made in the salient angle of any bastion, large rockets, weighing each from two to three hundred weight or more, and being each loaded with not less than a barrel of powder, are fired into the ruins after the revetment is broken, in order, by continual explosions, to render the breach practicable in the most expeditious way.

To insure every rocket that is fired having the desired effect, they are so heavily laden, as not to rise off the ground when fired along it; and under these circumstances are placed in a small shallow trench, run along to the foot of the glacis, from the nearest point of the third parallel, and in a direct line for the breach; by this means, the rockets being laid in this trench will invariably pursue exactly the same course, and every one of them will be infallibly lodged in the breach.

It is evident, that the whole of this is intended as a night operation, and a few hours would suffice, not only for running forward the trench, which need not be more than 18 inches deep, and about nine inches wide, undiscovered, but also for firing a sufficient number of rockets to make a most complete breach before the enemy could take means to prevent the combinations of the operation.

From the experiments I have lately made, I have reason to believe, that rockets much larger than those above mentioned may be formed for this description of service—rockets from half

Plate 9

Fig. 1

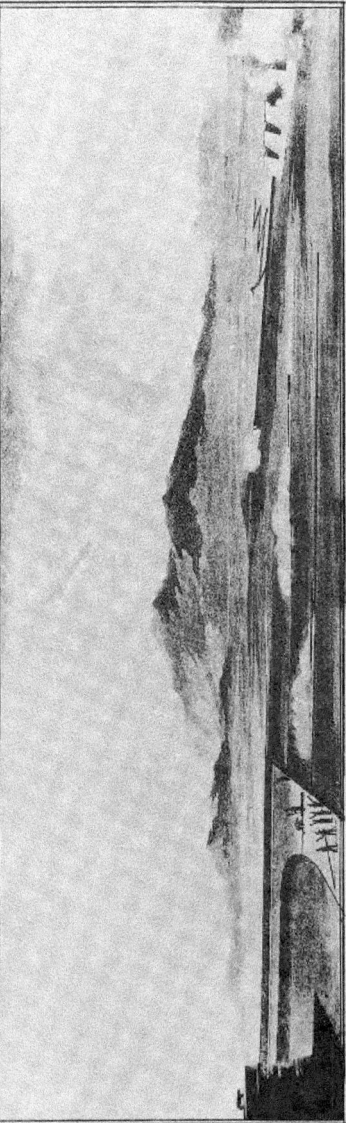

Fig. 2

a ton to a ton weight; which being driven in very strong and massive cast iron cases, may possess such strength and force, that, being fired by a process similar to that above described, even against the revetment of any fortress, unimpaired by a cannonade, it shall, by its mass and form, pierce the same; and having pierced it, shall, with one explosion of several barrels of powder, blow such portion of the masonry into the ditch, as shall, with very few rounds, complete a practicable breach.

It is evident, from this view of the weapon, that the Rocket System is not only capable of a degree of portability, and facility for light movements, which no weapon possesses. but that its ponderous parts, or the individual masses of its ammunition, also greatly exceed those of ordinary artillery. And yet, although this last description of rocket ammunition appears of an enormous mass, as ammunition, still if it be found capable of the powers here supposed, of which *I* have little doubt, the whole weight to be brought in this way against any town, for the accomplishment of a breach, will bear *no comparison* whatever to the weight of ammunition now required for the same service, independent of the saving of time and expense, and the great comparative simplicity of the approaches and works required for a siege carried on upon this system. This class of rockets I propose to denominate the *Belier a feù*.

Fig. 2 represents the converse of this system, or the use of these larger rockets for the defence of a fortress by the demolition of the batteries erected against it. In this case, the rockets are fired from embrasures, in the crest of the glacis, along trenches cut a part of the way in the direction of the works to be demolished.

Of the Use of Rockets by Infantry Against Cavalry, and in Covering the Storming of a Fortress

Plate 10, Fig. 1, represents an attack of cavalry against infantry, repulsed by the use of rockets. These rockets arc supposed to be of the lightest nature, 12 or 9-pounders, carried on bat horses or in small tumbrils, or with 6-pounder shell rockets, of which one man is capable of carrying six in a bundle, for any peculiar service; or so arranged, that the flank companies of every regiment may be armed, each man, with such a rocket, in addition to his carbine or rifle, the rocket being contained in a small leather case, attached to his cartouch, slinging the carbine or rifle, and carrying the stick on his shoulder, serving him either as a spear, by being made to receive the bayonet, or as a rest for his piece.

By this means every battalion would possess a powerful battery of this ammunition, *in addition* to all its ordinary means of attack and defence, and with scarcely any additional burthen to the flank companies, the whole weight of the rocket and stick not exceeding six pounds, and the difference between the weight of a rifle and that of a musket being about equivalent.

As to the mode of using them in action, for firing at long ranges, as these rockets are capable of a range of 2,000 yards, a few portable frames might be carried by each regiment, without any incumbrance, the frames for this description of rocket not being heavier than a musket; but as the true intention of the arm, in this distribution of it, is principally for close quarters, either in case of a charge of cavalry, or even of infantry, it is gen-

Plate 10

Fig. 1

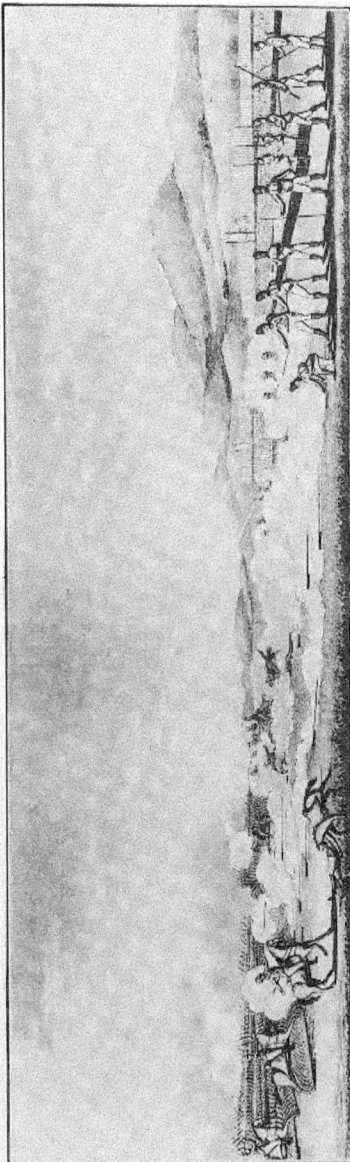

Fig. 2

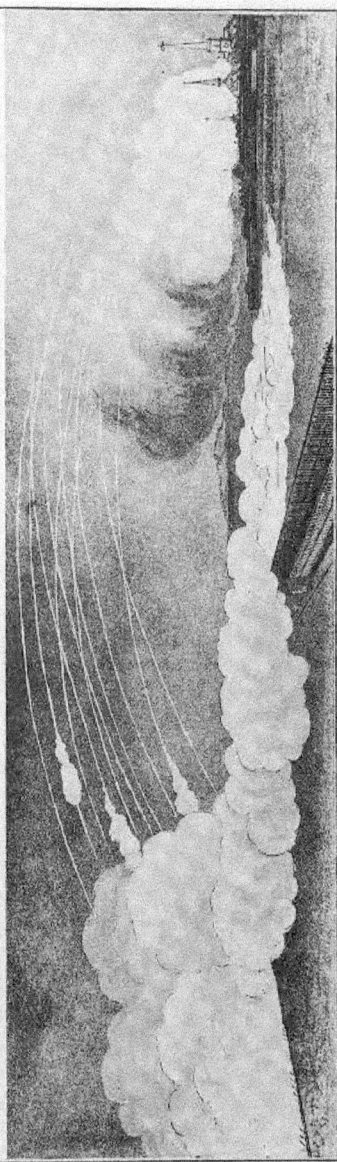

erally supposed to be fired in volleys, merely laid on the ground, as in the plate here described.

And, as it is well known, how successfully charges of cavalry are frequently sustained by infantry, even by the fire of the musket alone, it is not presuming too much to infer, that the repulse of cavalry would be *absolutely certain*, by masses of infantry, possessing the additional aid of powerful volleys of these shell rockets. So also, in charges of infantry, whether the battalion so armed be about to charge, or to receive a charge, a well-timed volley of one or two hundred such rockets, judiciously thrown in by the flank companies, must produce the most decisive effects.

Neither can it be doubted, that in advancing to an attack, the flank companies might make the most formidable use of this arm, mixed with the fire of their rifles or carbines, in all light infantry or *tiraillieur* manoeuvres. In like manner, in the passage of rivers, to protect the advanced party, or for the establishment of a *tête-du-pont*, and generally on all such occasions, rockets will be found capable of the greatest service, as shewn the other day in passing the Adour. In short, I must here remark that the use of the rocket, in these branches of it, is no more limited than the use of gunpowder itself.

Fig. 2 represents the covering of the storm of a fortified place by means of rockets. These are supposed to be of the heavy natures, both carcass and shell rockets; the former fired in great quantities from the trenches at high angles; the latter in ground ranges in front of the third parallel. It cannot be doubted that the confusion created in any place, by a fire of some thousand rockets thus thrown at two or three volleys quickly repeated, must be most favourable, either to the storming of a particular breach, or to a general escalade.

I must here observe, that although, in all cases, I lay the greatest stress upon the use of this arm in great quantities, it is not therefore to be presumed, that the effect of an individual rocket carcass, the smallest of which contains as much combustible matter as the 10-inch spherical carcass, is not at least equal to that of the 10-inch spherical carcass: or that the explosion of a shell thrown by a rocket, is not in its effects equal to the explosion of that same shell thrown by any other means: but that, as the power of *instantaneously* throwing the *most unlimited* quantities of carcasses or shells is the *exclusive property* of this weapon, and as there can be no question that an infinitely greater effect, both physical, as well as moral, is produced by the instantaneous application of any quantity of ammunition, with innumerable other advantages, than by a fire in slow succession of that same quantity.

So it would be an absolute absurdity, and a downright waste of power, not to make this exclusive property the general basis of every application of the weapon, limited only by a due proportion between the expenditure and the value of the object to be attained—a limit which I should always conceive it more advisable to exceed than to fall short of. (For a hundred fires breaking out at once, must necessarily produce more destruction than when they happen in succession, and may therefore be extinguished as fast as they occur.)

There is another most important use in this weapon, in the storming of fortified places, which should here be mentioned, *viz.* that as it is the only description of artillery ammunition that can ever be carried into a place by a storming party, and as, in fact, the heaviest rockets may accompany an escalade, so the value of it in these operations is infinite, and no escalade should ever be attempted without. It would enable the attackers, the moment they have got into the place, not only to scour the parapet most effectually, and to enfilade any street or passage where they may be opposed, and which they may wish to force; but even if thrown at random into the town, must distract the garrison, while it serves as a certain index to the different storming parties as to the situation and progress of each party.

The Use of Rockets from Boats

Plate 11 represents two men of war's launches throwing rockets. The frame is the same as that used for bombardment on shore, divested of the legs or prypoles, on which it is supported in land service; for which, afloat, the foremast of the boat is substituted. To render, therefore, the application of the common bombarding frame universal, each of them is constructed with a loop or traveller, to connect it with the mast, and guide it in lowering and raising, which is done by the haulyards.

The leading boat in the plate represents the act of firing; where the frame being elevated to any desired angle, the crew have retired into the stern sheets, and a marine artillery-man is discharging a rocket by a trigger-line, leading aft. In the second boat, these artillery-men are in the act of loading; for which purpose, the frame is lowered to a convenient height; the main-mast is also standing, and the mainsail set, but partly brailed up.

This sail being kept wet, most effectually prevents, without the least danger to the sail, any inconvenience to the men from the smoke or small sparks of the rocket when going off; it should, therefore, be used where no objection exists on account of wind. It is not, however, by any means indispensable, as I have myself discharged some hundred rockets from these, boats, nay, even from a six-oared cutter, without it. From this application of the sail, it is evident, that rockets may be thrown from these boats under sail, as well as at anchor, or in rowing. In the launch, the ammunition may be very securely stowed in the stern sheets, covered with tarpaulins, or tanned hides. In the six-oared cutter, there is not room for this, and an attending boat is therefore necessary: on which account, as well as from its greater steadiness, the launch is preferable, where there is no obstacle as to currents or shoal water.

Here it may be observed, with reference to its application in the marine, that as the power of discharging this ammunition without the burthen of ordnance, gives it exclusive facilities for land service, so also, its property of being projected without reaction upon the point of discharge, gives it exclusive facilities for sea service: insomuch, that rockets conveying the same quantity of combustible matter, as by the ordinary system would be thrown from the largest mortars, and from ships of very heavy tonnage, may be used out of the smallest boats of the navy; and the 12-pounder and 18-pounder have been frequently fired even from four-oared gigs.

It should here also be remarked, that the 12 and 18-pounder shell rockets *recochét* in the water remarkably well at low angles. There is another use for rockets in boat service also, which ought not to be passed over—namely, their application in facilitating the capture of a ship by boarding.

In this service 32-pounder shell rockets are prepared with a short stick, having a leader and short fuse fixed to the stick for firing the rocket. Thus prepared, every boat intended to board is provided with 10 or 12 of these rockets; the moment of coming alongside, the fuses are lighted, and the whole number of rockets immediately launched by hand through the ports into the ship; where, being left to their own impulse, they will scour round and round the deck until they explode, so as very shortly to clear the way for the boarders, both by actual destruction, and by the equally powerful operation of terror amongst the crew; the boat lying quietly alongside for a few seconds, until, by the explosion of the rockets, the boarders know that the desired effect has been produced, and that no mischief can happen to themselves when they enter the vessel.

Plate 11

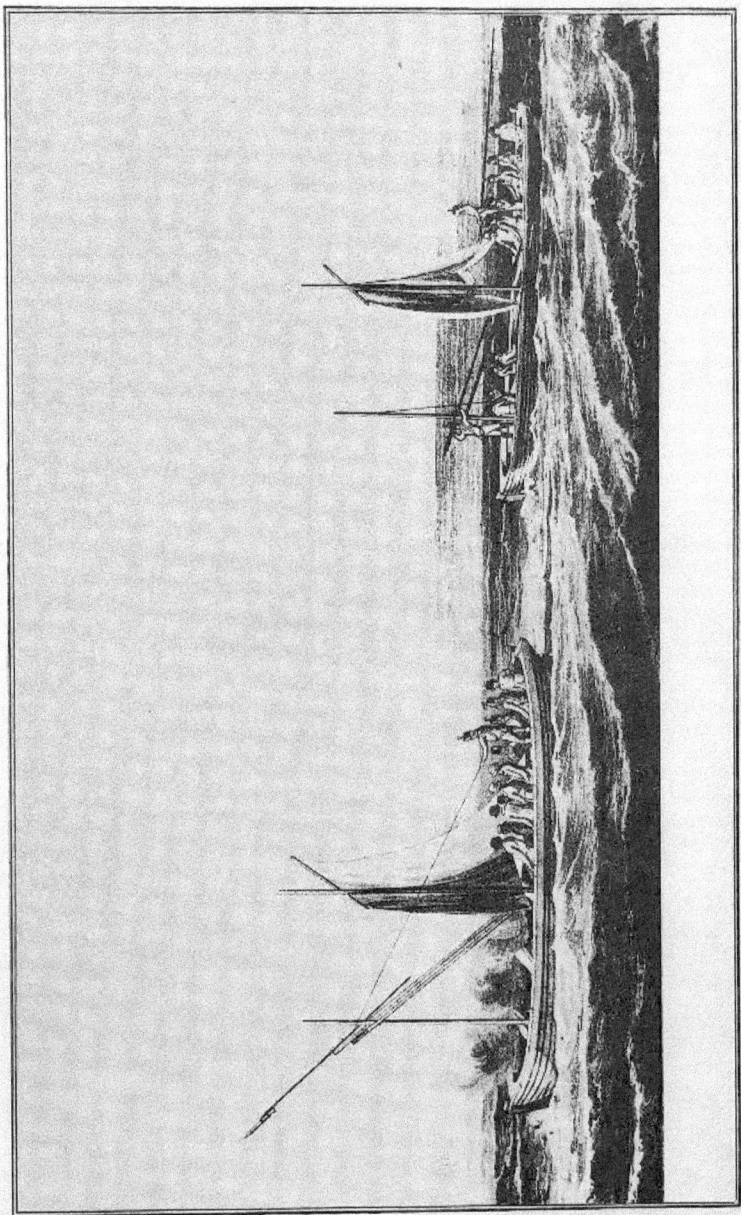

The Use of Rockets in Fire Ships, and the Mode of Fitting Any Other Ship for the Discharge of Rockets

Plate 12, Fig. 1, represents the application of rockets in fire ships; by which, a great power of distant conflagration is given to these ships, in addition to the limited powers they now possess, as depending entirely on contact with the vessels they may be intended to destroy.

The application is made as follows;—Frames or racks are to be provided in the tops of all fire-ships, to contain as many hundred carcass and shell rockets, as can be stowed in them, tier above tier, and nearly close together. These racks may also be applied in the topmast and top-gallant shrouds, to increase the number: and when the time arrives for sending her against the enemy, the rockets are placed in these racks, at different angles, and in all directions, having the vents uncovered, but requiring no leaders, or any nicety of operation, which can be frustrated either by wind or rain; as the rockets are discharged merely by the progress of the flame ascending the rigging, at a considerable lapse of time after the ship is set on fire, and abandoned.

It is evident, therefore, in the first place that no injury can happen to the persons charged with tarrying in the vessel, as they will have returned into safety before any discharge takes place. It is evident, also, that the most extensive destruction to the enemy may be calculated on, as the discharge will commence about the time that the fireship has drifted in amongst the enemies' ships: when issuing in the most tremendous volleys, the smallest ship being supposed not to have less than 1,000 rockets, distributed in different directions, it is impossible but that every ship of the enemy must, with fire-ships enough, and no stint of rockets, be covered sooner or later with clouds of this destructive fire; whereas, without this distant power of destruction, it is ten to one if every fire-ship does not pass harmlessly through the fleet, by the exertions of the enemies' boats in towing them clear.

Exertions, it must be remarked, entirely precluded in this system of fire-ships, as it is impossible that any boat could venture to approach a vessel so equipped, and pouring forth shell and carcass rockets, in all directions, and at all angles. I had an opportunity of trying this experiment in the attack of the French Fleet in Basque Roads, and though on a very small scale indeed, it was ascertained, that the greatest confusion and terror was created by it in the enemy.

Figs. 2, 3, and 4, represent the mode of fitting any ship to fire rockets, from scuttles in her broadside; giving, thereby, to every vessel having a between-deck, a rocket battery, in addition to the gun batteries on her spar deck, without the one interfering in the smallest degree with the other, or without the least risk to the ship; the sparks of the rocket in going off being completely excluded, either by iron shutters closing the scuttle from within, as practised in the *Galgo* defence ship, fitted with 21 rocket scuttles in her broadside, as shewn in Fig. 3. Or by a particular construction of scuttle and frame which I have since devised, and applied to the *Erebus* sloop of war: so that the whole of the scuttle is completely filled, in all positions of traverse, and at all angles, by the frame; and thereby any possibility of the entrance of fire completely prevented.

In both these ships, the rockets may be either discharged at the highest angles, for bombardment, or used at low angles, as an additional means of offence or defence against other shipping in action; as the rockets, thus used, are capable of projecting 18-pounder shot, or 4½-inch shells, or even 24-pounder solid shot. This arrangement literally gives the description of small vessels here mentioned, a second and most powerful deck, for

Plate 12

Fig. 1

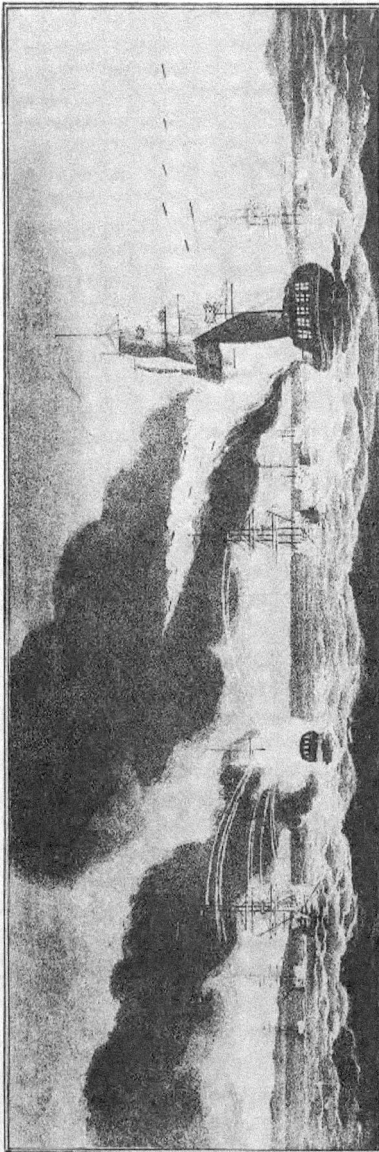

Fig. 3.

Fig. 2

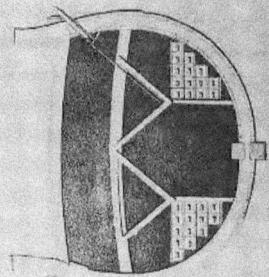

Fig. 4

general service as well as for bombardment.

Smaller vessels, such as gun brigs, schooners, and cutters, may be fitted to fire rockets by frames, similar to the boat frames, described in Plate 11, from their spar deck, and either over the, broadside, or the stern; their frames being arranged to travel up and down, on a small upright spar or boat's mast, fixed perpendicularly to the outside of the bulwark of the vessel.

As a temporary expedient, or in small vessels, this mode answer very well: but it has the objection of not carrying the sparks so far from the rigging, as when fired from below: it interferes also with the fighting the guns at the same time, and can therefore only be applied exclusively in the case of bombardment. All the gun brigs, however, on the Boulogne station, during Commodore Owen's command there, were fitted in this manner, some with two and some with three frames on a broadside.

Rocket Ammunition

Plate 13 represents all the different natures of rocket ammunition which have hitherto been made, from the eight-inch carcass or explosion rocket, weighing nearly three hundred weight, to the six-pounder shell rocket, and shews the comparative dimensions of the whole.

This ammunition may be divided into three parts—the heavy, medium, and light natures. The heavy natures are those denominated by the number of inches in their diameter; the medium from the 42-pounder to the 24-pounder inclusive; and the light natures from the 18-pounder to the 6-pounder inclusive.

The ranges of the eight-inch, seven-inch, and six-inch rockets, are from 2,000 to 2,500 yards; and the quantities of combustible matter, or bursting powder, from 25 lbs. and upwards to 50 lbs. Their sticks are divided into four parts, secured with ferules, and carried in the angles of the packing case, containing the rocket, one rocket in each case, so that notwithstanding the length of the stick, the whole of this heavy part of the system possesses, in proportion, the same facility as the medium and light parts.

These rockets are fired from bombarding frames, similar to those of the 42- and 32-pounder carcasses; or they may be fired from a slope of earth in the same way. They may also be fired along the ground, as explained in Plate 9, for the purposes of explosion.

These large rockets have from their weight, combined with less diameter, even more penetration than the heaviest shells, and are therefore equally efficient for the destruction of bomb

Plate 13

Fig 1

Fig 2

Fig 3

Fig 4

Fig 5

Fig 6

Fig 7

Fig 8

Fig 9

Eight Inch Carcase or Explosion Rocket

Seven Inch Carcase or Explosion Rocket

Six Inch Carcase or Explosion Rocket

32 Pounder Carcase

32 Pounder Carcase

32 Pounder Shell

24 Pounder Shell

24 Pounder Case Shot

18 Pounder Shell

18 Pounder Case Shot

12 Pounder Shell

12 Pounder Case Shot

9 Pounder Shell

9 Pounder Case Shot

6 Pounder Shell

Fig 14

Fig 13

Fig 12

Fig 11

Fig 10

Fig 15

proofs, or the demolition of strong buildings; and their construction having now been realised, it is proved that the facilities of the rocket system are not its only excellence, but that it actually will propel heavier masses than can be done by any other means; that is to say, masses, to project which, it would be scarcely possible to cast, much less to transport, mortars of sufficient magnitude. Various modifications of the powers of these large rockets may be made, which it is not necessary here to specify.

The 42- and 32-pounders are those which have hitherto been principally used in bombardment, and which, for the general purposes of bombardment, will be found sufficient, while their portability renders them in that respect more easily applied. I have therefore classed them as medium rockets. These rockets will convey from ten to seven pounds of combustible matter each; have a range of upwards of 3,000 yards; and may, where the fall of greater mass in any particular spot is required, either for penetration or increased fire, be discharged in combinations of three, four, or six rockets, well lashed together, with the sticks in the centre also strongly, bound together.

The great art of firing these *fasces of rockets* is to arrange them, so that they may be sure to take fire contemporaneously, which must be done either by priming the bottoms of all thoroughly, or by firing them by a flash of powder, which is sure to ignite the whole combination at once. The 42- and 32-pounder rockets may also be used as explosion rockets, and the 32-poundrr armed with shot or shells: thus, a 32-pounder will range at least 1,000 yards, laid on the ground, and armed with a 5½-inch howitzer shell, or an 18 and even a 24-pounder solid shot.

The 32-pounder is, as it were, the mean point of the system: it is the least rocket used as a carcass in bombardment, and the largest armed either with shot or shell, for field service. The 24-pounder rocket is very nearly equal to it in all its applications in the field; from the saving of weight, therefore, I consider it preferable. It is perfectly equal to propel the cohorn shell or 12-pounder shot.

The 18-pounder, which is the first of the *light* natures of rockets, is armed with a 9-pounder shot or shell; the 12-pounder

87

with a 6-pounder *ditto*; the 9-pounder with a grenade; and the 6-pounder with a 3-pounder shot or shell. These shells, however, are now cast expressly for the rocket service, and are elliptical instead of spherical, thereby increasing the power of the shell, and decreasing the resistance of the air.

From the 24-pounder to the 9-pounder rocket, inclusive, a description of case shot rocket is formed of each nature, armed with a quantity of musket or carbine balls, put into the top of the cylinder of the rocket, and from thence discharged by a quantity of powder contained in a chamber, by which the velocity of these balls, when in flight, is increased beyond that of the rocket's motion, an effect which cannot be given in the spherical case, where the bursting powder only liberates the balls.

All rockets intended for explosion, whether the powder be contained in a wrought iron head or cone, as used in bombardment: or whether in the shell above mentioned, for field service, or in the case shot, are fitted with an external fuse of paper, which is ignited from the vent at the moment when the rocket is fired. These fuses may be instantaneously cut to any desired length, from 25 seconds downwards, by a pair of common scissors or nippers, and communicate to the bursting charge, by a quickmatch, in a small tube on the outside of the rocket.

In the shell rocket the paper fuse communicates with a wooden fuse in the shell, which, being cut to the shortest length that can be necessary, is never required to be taken out of the shell, but is regulated either by taking away the paper fuse altogether, or leaving any part of it, which, in addition to the fixed and permanent wooden fuse in the shell, may make up the whole time of flight required. By this system, the arrangement of the fuse in action is intended with a facility, security, and an expedition, not known in any other similar operations.

All the rocket sticks for land service are made in parts of convenient length for carriage, and jointed by iron ferules. For sea services they are made in the whole length.

The 24-pounder shell and case shot rockets are those which I propose issuing in future for the heavy field carriages; the 18-pounder shell and case shot for the light field carriages; the

12-pounder for the mounted ammunition of cavalry; the 9- and 6-pounders for infantry, according to the different cases already explained.

Fig. 1, 2, 3, 4, 5, 6. 7, 8. and 9, represent the different implements used for jointing the sticks, or fixing them to the rocket, being of different sizes, in proportion to the different natures to which they belong. They consist of hammers, pincers, vices, and wrenches, all to accomplish the same object, namely, that of compressing the ferule into the stick, by means of strong steel points in the tool, so as to fix it immovably. The varieties are here all shewn, because I have not hitherto decided which is the preferable instrument.

Fig. 10, 11, 12, and 13, represent another mode of arranging the different natures of ammunition, which is hitherto merely a matter of speculation, but which may in certain parts of the system be hereafter found a considerable improvement. It is the carrying the rocket, or projectile force, distinct from the ammunition itself, instead of combining them in their first construction, as hitherto supposed.

Thus, Fig. 10 is the rocket, and Fig. 11, 12, and 13, are respectively a shell, case shot, or carcass, which may be immediately fixed to the rocket by a screw, according as either the one or the other nature is required at the time. A greater variety of ammunition might thus be carried for particular services, with a less burthen altogether.

Fig. 14 and 15 represent the right ball or floating carcass rocket. This is supposed to be a 42-pounder rocket, containing in its head, as in Fig. 12, a parachute with a light ball or carcass attached to it by a slight chain. This rocket being fired nearly perpendicularly into the air, the head is burst off at its greatest altitude, by a very small explosion, which, though it ignites the light ball, does not injure the parachute; but by liberating it from the rocket, leaves it suspended in the air, as Fig.13, in which situation, as a light ball, it will continue to give a very brilliant light, illuminating the atmosphere for nearly ten minutes; or as a carcass, in a tolerable breeze, will float in the air, and convey the fire for several miles, unperceived and unconsumed, if only the match of the carcass be ignited at the disengagement of the parachute.

It should be observed that, with due care, the rocket ammunition is not only the most secure, but the most durable that can be: every rocket is, in fact, a charge of powder hermetically sealed in a metal case, impervious either to the ordinary accidents by fire, or damage from humidity. I have used rockets that had been three years on board of ship, without any apparent loss of power; and when after a certain period, which, from my present experience, I cannot estimate at less than eight or ten years, their force shall have so far suffered as to render them unserviceable, they may again be regenerated, at the mere expense of boring out the composition and re-driving it: the stick, case, &c. that is to say, all the principal parts, being as serviceable as ever.

The ranges of these different natures of rocket ammunition are shown on the following page.

The Ranges of these different Natures of Rocket Ammunition are as follow:

Nature of Rocket.	Point Blank, or Ground Practice.	20 to 25°	25 to 30°	30 to 35°	35 to 40°	40 to 45°	45 to 50°	50 to 55°	55 to 66°	60 to 65°	Elevation. Ranges.
	Yards.	Yards.	Yards.	Yards.	Yards.	Yards.	Yards.	Yards.	Yards.	Yards.	
6, 7, and 8 Inch..	....	....	....	....	....	....	....	....	....	2,100 to 2,500	
42-Pounder	....	....	....	....	....	....	....	2,000 to 2,500	2,500 to 3,000		
32-Pounder	1,000 to 1,200	....	....	1,000 to 1,500	1,500 to 2,000	2,000 to 2,500	2,500 to 3,000	3,000 to 3,200			
24-Pounder	nearly the same ranges.						2,500				
18-Pounder	1,000		1,000 to 1,500	1,500 ..... to	2,000 .... to	2,000 ..... to					
12-Pounder	nearly the same.										
9-Pounder	800 to 1,000		1,500 .... and	upwards.	2,000 ..... to	2,200					
6-Pounder	nearly the same.	1,000 to 1,500									

Conclusion

CALCULATIONS PROVING THE COMPARATIVE ECONOMY OF THE ROCKET AMMUNITION, BOTH AS TO ITS APPLICATION IN BOMBARDMENT AND IN THE FIELD

So much misapprehension having been entertained with regard to the expense of the rocket system, it is very important, for the true understanding of the weapon, to prove, that it is by far the cheapest mode of applying artillery ammunition, both in bombardment and in the field.

To begin with the expense of making the 32-pounder rocket carcass, which has hitherto been principally used in bombardments, compared with the 10-inch carcass, which conveys even less combustible matter.

		£.	s.	d.
	Case	0	5	0
Cost of a 32-pounder / Cone		0	2	11
Rocket Carcass, complete / Stick		0	2	6
for firing in the present / Rocket composition		0	3	9
mode of manufacture. / Carcass ditto		0	2	3
	Labour, paint, &c.	0	5	6
		£1	1	11

If the construction were more systematic, and elementary force used instead of manual labour, the expense of driving the rocket might be reduced four-fifths, which would lower the amount to about 18s. each rocket, complete; and if bamboo were substituted, which I am endeavouring to accomplish, for the stick, the whole expense of each 32-pounder carcass rocket would be about 16s. each.

Now as the calculation of the expense of the rocket includes that of the projectile force, which conveys it 3,000 yards; to equalize the comparison, to the cost of the spherical carcass must be added that of the charge of powder required to convey it the same distance.

		£.	s.	d.
Cost of a 10-inch Spherical Carcass, with a proportionate charge of powder, &c.	Value of a 10-inch spherical carcass..........	0	15	7
	Ditto of charge of powder, to range it 3,000 yards	0	6	0
	Cartridge tube, &c.	0	1	0
		£1	2	7

So that even with the present disadvantages of manufacture, there is an actual saving in the 32-pounder rocket carcass itself, which contains more composition than the 10-inch spherical carcass, *without allowing anything for the difference of expense of the rocket apparatus, and that of the mortar, mortar beds, platforms, &c.* which, together with the difficulty of transport, constitute the greatest expense of throwing the common carcass; whereas, the cost of apparatus for the use of the rocket carcass does not originally exceed £5.

And indeed, on most occasions, the rocket may, as has been shewn, be thrown even without any apparatus at all: besides which, it may be stated, that a transport of 200 tons will convey 5,000 rocket carcasses, with everything required for using them, on a very extensive scale; while on shore, a common ammunition waggon will carry 60 rounds, with the requisites for action. The difference in all these respects, as to the 10-inch spherical carcass, its mortars, &c. is too striking to need specifying.

But the comparison as to expense is still more in favour of the rocket, when compared with the larger natures of carcasses. The 13-inch spherical carcass costs £1. 17s. 11½d. to throw it 2,500 yards; the 32-pounder rocket carcass, conveying the same quantity of combustible matter, does not cost more than £1. 5s. 0d.—so that in this case there is a saving on the first cost of 12s. 11½d. Now the large rocket carcass requires no more apparatus than the small one, and the difference of weight, as to carriage, is little more than that of the different quantities of combustible matter contained in each, while the difference of weight of the 13-inch and 10-inch carcasses is at least double, as is also that of the mortars; and, consequently, all the other comparative charges are enhanced in the same proportion.

In like manner, the 42-pounder carcass rocket, which contains from 15 to 18 lbs. of combustible matter, will be found considerably cheaper in the first cost than the 13-inch spherical carcass: and a proportionate economy, including the ratio of increased effect, will attach also to the still larger natures of rockets which I have now made. Thus, the first cost of the 6-inch rocket, weighing 150 lbs. and containing 40 lbs. of combustible matter, is not more than £3. 10s. that is to say, less than double the first cost of the 13-inch spherical carcass, though its conflagrating powers, or the quantity of combustible matter conveyed by it, are three times as great, and its mass and penetration are half as much again as that of the 10-inch shell or carcass.

It is evident, therefore, that however extended the magnitude of rockets may be, and I am now endeavouring to construct some, the falling mass of which will be considerably more than that of the 13-inch shell or carcass, and whose powers, therefore, either of explosion or conflagration, will rise even in a higher ratio, still, although the first cost may exceed that of any projectile at present thrown, on a comparison of effects, there will be a great saving in favour of the Rocket System.

It is difficult to make a precise calculation as to the average expense of every common shell or carcass, actually thrown against the enemy; but it is generally supposed and admitted, that, on a moderate estimate, these missiles, one with another, cannot cost government less than £5 each; nor can this be doubted, when, in addition to the first cost of the ammunition, that of the *ordnance, and the charges incidental to its application*, are considered.

But as to the rocket and its apparatus, it has been seen, that the principal expense is that of the first construction, an expense, which it must be fairly stated, that the charges of conveyance cannot more than double under any circumstances; so that where the mode of throwing carcasses by 32-pounder rockets is adopted, there is, at least, an average saving of £3 on every carcass so thrown, and proportionally for the larger natures; especially as not only the conflagrating powers of the spherical carcass are equalled even by the 32-pounder rocket, but greatly exceeded by the larger rockets; and the move especially indeed, as the difference of accuracy, for the purposes of bombardment, is not worthy to be mentioned, since it is no uncommon thing for shells fired from a mortar at long ranges, to spread to the right and left of each other, upwards of 500 or even 600 yards, as was lately proved by a series of experiments, where the mortar bed was actually fixed in the ground.

An aberration which the rocket will never equal, unless some accident happens to the stick in firing; and this, I may venture to say, does not occur oftener than the failure of the fuse in the firing of shells. The fact is, that whatever aberration does exist in the rocket, it is distinctly seen; whereas, in ordinary projectiles it is scarcely to be traced—and hence has arisen a very exaggerated notion of the inaccuracy of the former.

But to recur to the economy of the rocket carcass; how much is not the saving of this system of bombardment enhanced, when considered with reference to naval bombardment, when the expensive construction of the large mortar vessel is viewed, together with the charge of their whole establishment, compared with the few occasions of their use, and their unfitness for general service? Whereas, by means of the rocket, every vessel, nay, every boat, has the power of throwing carcasses without any alteration in her construction, or any impediment whatever to her general services.

So much for the comparison required as to the application of the rocket in bombardment; I shall now proceed to the calculation of the expense of this ammunition for field service, compared with that of common artillery ammunition. In the first place, it should be stated that the rocket will project every species of shot or shell which can be fired from field guns, and indeed, even heavier ammunition than is ordinarily used by artillery in the field. But it will be a fair criterion to make the calculation, with reference to the six and nine-pounder common ammunition; these two natures of shot or shell are projected by a small rocket, which I have denominated the 12-pounder, and which will give horizontally, and *without apparatus*, the same range as that of the gun, and *with apparatus*, considerably more. The calculation may be stated as follows:—

		£.	s.	d.
12-pounder Rocket	Case and stick	0	5	6
	Rocket composition	0	1	10½
	Labour, &c.	0	2	0
		£0	9	4½

But this sum is capable of the following reduction, by substituting elementary force for manual labour, and by employing bamboo in lieu of the stick.

		£.	s.	d.
* Reduced Price	Case and stick	0	4	0
	Composition	0	1	10½
	Driving	0	0	6
		£0	6	4½

★And this is the sum that ought to be taken in general calculation of the advantages of which the system is *capable*, because to this it *may* be brought.

Now the cost of the shot or spherical case is the same whether projected from a gun or thrown by the rocket; and the fixing it to the rocket costs about the same as strapping the shot to the wooden bottom.

This 6*s*. 4½*d*. therefore is to be set against the value of the gunpowder, cartridge, &c. required for the gun, which may be estimated as follows:—

		£.	s.	d.
6-pounder Ammⁿ.	Charge of powder for the 6-pounder	0	2	0
	Cartridge, 3½*d*. wooden bottom, 2½*d*. and tube, 1¼*d*.	0	0	7¼
		£0	2	7¼

		£.	s.	d.
9-pounder Ammⁿ.	For the 9-pounder charge of powder	0	3	0
	Cartridge, 4½*d*. wooden bottom, 2½*d*. and tube, 1¼*d*.	0	0	8¼
		£0	3	8¼

Taking the average, therefore, of the six and nine-pounder ammunition, the rocket ammunition costs 3s. 2¾d. a round more than the common ammunition.

Now we must compare the simplicity of the use of the rocket, with the expensive apparatus of artillery, to see what this trifling difference of first cost in the rocket has to weigh against it. In the first place, we have seen, that in many situations the rocket requires no apparatus at all to use it, and that, where it does require any, it is of the simplest kind: we have seen also, that both infantry and cavalry can, in a variety of instances, combine this weapon with their other powers; so that it is not, in such cases, *even to be charged with the pay of the men.*

These, however, are circumstances that can *in no case* happen with respect to ordinary artillery ammunition; the use of which never can be divested of the expense of the construction, transport, and maintenance of the necessary ordnance to project it, or of the men *exclusively* required to work that ordnance. What proportion, therefore, will the trifling difference of first cost, and the average facile and inexpensive application of the rocket bear to the heavy contingent charges involved in the use of field artillery?

It is a fact, that, in the famous Egyptian campaign, those charges did not amount to less than £20 per round, one with another, *exclusive* of the pay of the men; nor can they for any campaign be put at less than from £2 to £3 per round. It must be obvious, therefore, although it is not perhaps practicable actually to clothe the calculation in figures, that the saving must be very great indeed in favour of the rocket, in the field as well as in bombardment.

Thus far, however, the calculation is limited merely as to the bare question of expense; but on the score of general advantage, how is not the balance augmented in favour of the rocket, when all the *exclusive* facilities of its use are taken into the account— the *universality* of the application, the *unlimited* quantity of instantaneous fire to be produced by it for particular occasions— of fire not to be by any possibility approached in quantity by means of ordnance? Now to all these points of excellence one only drawback is attempted to be stated—this is, the difference of accuracy: but the value of the objection vanishes when fairly considered; for in the first place, it must be admitted, that the general business of action is not that of target-firing; and the more especially with a weapon like the rocket, which possesses the facility of bringing such quantities of fire on any point: thus, if the difference of accuracy were as ten to one against the rocket, as the facility of using it is at least as ten to one in its favour, the ratio would be that of equality.

The truth is, however, that the difference of accuracy, for actual application against troops, instead of ten to one, cannot be stated even as two to one; and, consequently, the compound ratio as to effect, the same shot or shell being projected, would be, even with this admission of comparative inaccuracy, greatly in favour of the Rocket System.

But it must still further be borne in mind, that this system is yet in its infancy, that much has been accomplished in a short time, and that there is every reason to believe, that the accuracy of the rocket may be actually brought upon a par with that of other artillery ammunition for all the important purposes of field service.

W. Congreve.

LEONAUR

ALSO FROM LEONAUR
AVAILABLE IN SOFTCOVER OR HARDCOVER WITH DUST JACKET

THE FALL OF THE MOGHUL EMPIRE OF HINDUSTAN *by H. G. Keene*—By the beginning of the nineteenth century, as British and Indian armies under Lake and Wellesley dominated the scene, a little over half a century of conflict brought the Moghul Empire to its knees.

LADY SALE'S AFGHANISTAN *by Florentia Sale*—An Indomitable Victorian Lady's Account of the Retreat from Kabul During the First Afghan War.

THE CAMPAIGN OF MAGENTA AND SOLFERINO 1859 *by Harold Carmichael Wylly*—The Decisive Conflict for the Unification of Italy.

FRENCH'S CAVALRY CAMPAIGN *by J. G. Maydon*—A Special Correspondent's View of British Army Mounted Troops During the Boer War.

CAVALRY AT WATERLOO *by Sir Evelyn Wood*—British Mounted Troops During the Campaign of 1815.

THE SUBALTERN *by George Robert Gleig*—The Experiences of an Officer of the 85th Light Infantry During the Peninsular War.

NAPOLEON AT BAY, 1814 *by F. Loraine Petre*—The Campaigns to the Fall of the First Empire.

NAPOLEON AND THE CAMPAIGN OF 1806 *by Colonel Vachée*—The Napoleonic Method of Organisation and Command to the Battles of Jena & Auerstädt.

THE COMPLETE ADVENTURES IN THE CONNAUGHT RANGERS *by William Grattan*—The 88th Regiment during the Napoleonic Wars by a Serving Officer.

BUGLER AND OFFICER OF THE RIFLES *by William Green & Harry Smith*—With the 95th (Rifles) during the Peninsular & Waterloo Campaigns of the Napoleonic Wars.

NAPOLEONIC WAR STORIES *by Sir Arthur Quiller-Couch*—Tales of soldiers, spies, battles & sieges from the Peninsular & Waterloo campaingns.

CAPTAIN OF THE 95TH (RIFLES) *by Jonathan Leach*—An officer of Wellington's sharpshooters during the Peninsular, South of France and Waterloo campaigns of the Napoleonic wars.

RIFLEMAN COSTELLO *by Edward Costello*—The adventures of a soldier of the 95th (Rifles) in the Peninsular & Waterloo Campaigns of the Napoleonic wars.

LEONAUR

ALSO FROM LEONAUR
AVAILABLE IN SOFTCOVER OR HARDCOVER WITH DUST JACKET

ESCAPE FROM THE FRENCH *by Edward Boys*—A Young Royal Navy Midshipman's Adventures During the Napoleonic War.

THE VOYAGE OF H.M.S. PANDORA *by Edward Edwards R. N. & George Hamilton, edited by Basil Thomson*—In Pursuit of the Mutineers of the Bounty in the South Seas—1790-1791.

MEDUSA *by J. B. Henry Savigny and Alexander Correard and Charlotte-Adélaïde Dard* —Narrative of a Voyage to Senegal in 1816 & The Sufferings of the Picard Family After the Shipwreck of the Medusa.

THE SEA WAR OF 1812 VOLUME 1 *by A. T. Mahan*—A History of the Maritime Conflict.

THE SEA WAR OF 1812 VOLUME 2 *by A. T. Mahan*—A History of the Maritime Conflict.

WETHERELL OF H. M. S. HUSSAR *by John Wetherell*—The Recollections of an Ordinary Seaman of the Royal Navy During the Napoleonic Wars.

THE NAVAL BRIGADE IN NATAL *by C. R. N. Burne*—With the Guns of H. M. S. Terrible & H. M. S. Tartar during the Boer War 1899-1900.

THE VOYAGE OF H. M. S. BOUNTY *by William Bligh*—The True Story of an 18th Century Voyage of Exploration and Mutiny.

SHIPWRECK! *by William Gilly*—The Royal Navy's Disasters at Sea 1793-1849.

KING'S CUTTERS AND SMUGGLERS: 1700-1855 *by E. Keble Chatterton*—A unique period of maritime history-from the beginning of the eighteenth to the middle of the nineteenth century when British seamen risked all to smuggle valuable goods from wool to tea and spirits from and to the Continent.

CONFEDERATE BLOCKADE RUNNER *by John Wilkinson*—The Personal Recollections of an Officer of the Confederate Navy.

NAVAL BATTLES OF THE NAPOLEONIC WARS *by W. H. Fitchett*—Cape St. Vincent, the Nile, Cadiz, Copenhagen, Trafalgar & Others.

PRISONERS OF THE RED DESERT *by R. S. Gwatkin-Williams*—The Adventures of the Crew of the Tara During the First World War.

U-BOAT WAR 1914-1918 *by James B. Connolly/Karl von Schenk*—Two Contrasting Accounts from Both Sides of the Conflict at Sea D uring the Great War.

LEONAUR

ALSO FROM LEONAUR
AVAILABLE IN SOFTCOVER OR HARDCOVER WITH DUST JACKET

A DIARY FROM DIXIE *by Mary Boykin Chesnut*—A Lady's Account of the Confederacy During the American Civil War

FOLLOWING THE DRUM *by Teresa Griffin Vielé*—A U. S. Infantry Officer's Wife on the Texas frontier in the Early 1850's

FOLLOWING THE GUIDON *by Elizabeth B. Custer*—The Experiences of General Custer's Wife with the U. S. 7th Cavalry.

LADIES OF LUCKNOW *by G. Harris & Adelaide Case*—The Experiences of Two British Women During the Indian Mutiny 1857. A Lady's Diary of the Siege of Lucknow by G. Harris, Day by Day at Lucknow by Adelaide Case

MARIE-LOUISE AND THE INVASION OF 1814 *by Imbert de Saint-Amand*— The Empress and the Fall of the First Empire

SAPPER DOROTHY *by Dorothy Lawrence*—The only English Woman Soldier in the Royal Engineers 51st Division, 79th Tunnelling Co. during the First World War

ARMY LETTERS FROM AN OFFICER'S WIFE 1871-1888 *by Frances M. A. Roe*—Experiences On the Western Frontier With the United States Army

NAPOLEON'S LETTERS TO JOSEPHINE *by Henry Foljambe Hall*—Correspondence of War, Politics, Family and Love 1796-1814

MEMOIRS OF SARAH DUCHESS OF MARLBOROUGH, AND OF THE COURT OF QUEEN ANNE VOLUME 1 by A. T. Thomson

MEMOIRS OF SARAH DUCHESS OF MARLBOROUGH, AND OF THE COURT OF QUEEN ANNE VOLUME 2 by A. T. Thomson

MARY PORTER GAMEWELL AND THE SIEGE OF PEKING *by A. H. Tuttle*—An American Lady's Experiences of the Boxer Uprising, China 1900

VANISHING ARIZONA *by Martha Summerhayes*—A young wife of an officer of the U.S. 8th Infantry in Apacheria during the 1870's

THE RIFLEMAN'S WIFE *by Mrs. Fitz Maurice*—*The Experiences of an Officer's Wife and Chronicles of the Old 95th During the Napoleonic Wars*

THE OATMAN GIRLS *by Royal B. Stratton*—The Capture & Captivity of Two Young American Women in the 1850's by the Apache Indians

www.ingramcontent.com/pod-product-compliance
Lightning Source LLC
Chambersburg PA
CBHW020506100426
42813CB00030B/3146/J